# PASS THE LOOT

## A Fox Trot Collection
by Bill Amend
Foreword by Lynn Johnston

**Andrews and McMeel**     A Universal Press Syndicate Company     **Kansas City**

**FOX TROT** is syndicated internationally by Universal Press Syndicate.

**Pass the Loot** copyright © 1990 by Universal Press Syndicate. All rights reserved. Printed in the United States of America. No part of this book may be used or reproduced in any manner whatsoever without written permission except in the context of reviews. For information write Andrews and McMeel, a Universal Press Syndicate Company, 4900 Main Street, Kansas City, Missouri 64112.

ISBN: 0-8362-1815-9

Library of Congress Catalog Card Number: 89-82506

First Printing, June 1990
Sixth Printing, October 1994

## Foreword

They say there's no competition in this business—but nothing makes a cartoonist work harder than a brand-new strip that's written well and drawn well and fairly knocks your socks off!

Bill Amend's Fox Trot is frustratingly funny. He keeps writing stuff I wish I'd written. He keeps drawing stuff I wish I'd drawn.

They say there's no competition in this business, but Bill Amend is making a lot of us work harder. We're all trying to draw comics. . .while looking for our socks.

—Lynn Johnston

To Mark, Nicole and Rich

6

by Bill Amend

# FoxTrot

**WHAT'S WITH HIM?**

**I DUNNO, BUT HE'S GOT THAT "MARCH TO THE GALLOWS" LOOK.**

**DAD, I'VE DONE SOMETHING HORRIBLE.**

**WHAT IS IT, SON?**

**SOMETHING TERRIBLE.**

**I'M GLAD YOU'RE COMING TO ME. YOU WANT TO TELL ME ABOUT IT?**

**I'M NOT SURE YOU'LL EVER LOOK AT ME THE SAME AGAIN.**

**DON'T BE RIDICULOUS. WHAT'D YOU DO?**

SPRINGSTEEN TO TOUR WITH CARTOONIST
Dream Come True "says Boss

AMEND

**I MADE A MISTAKE. I MADE A HUGE MISTAKE. I JUST WASN'T THINKING.**

**JASON, EVERYONE MAKES MISTAKES. WHAT'S IMPORTANT IS YOU'RE FESSING UP TO IT. NOW, WHAT'D YOU DO?**

**I GOT A "B" ON MY MATH TEST.**

**A "B."**

**I FEEL SO...SO COMMON.**

**BELIEVE ME, JASON...**

9

CAN I STAY OVER AT STEVE'S TONIGHT?

I SUPPOSE SO.

IS IT OK IF I SLEEP OVER AT MARCUS'?

SURE.

NICOLE WANTS ME TO STAY OVER AT HER HOUSE TONIGHT.

THAT'S FINE.

DARE I ASK?

AMEND

WELL, IT LOOKS LIKE IT'S JUST YOU AND ME TONIGHT. THE KIDS ARE ALL STAYING WITH FRIENDS.

YOU AND ME, ALONE? FOR A WHOLE NIGHT?

I THOUGHT WE MIGHT SPEND A QUIET EVENING CUDDLING IN FRONT OF THE TV.

I'D LIKE THAT.

AMEND

WE COULD MAKE SOME POPCORN... GET A BLANKET OUT OF THE CLOSET...

I'D LIKE THAT A LOT.

YOU WOULD? REALLY?

ABSOLUTELY. THE LAKERS GAME IS ON IN 20 MINUTES.

I HAVE AN IDEA. WHY DON'T WE RENT A MOVIE THEN SNUGGLE UP AND WATCH IT?

WHAT ABOUT THE LAKERS GAME?

TOUGH PATOOTIES.

WHAT'S THAT SUPPOSED TO MEAN?

INTERPRET IT AS YOU WILL.

AMEND

HOW'S "AN AMERICAN IN PARIS" SOUND?

EXCUSE ME— WHAT'S A PATOOTIE?

CAN I FEED QUINCY?

SURE. THERE ARE SOME WORMS IN THE TUB UNDER MY BED.

WHAT TUB?

THE OLD CARAMEL CORN ONE.

THERE'S NO CARAMEL CORN TUB UNDER HERE...

CARAMEL CORN? I LOVE CARAMEL CORN!

THE LITTLE BRAT'S BEEN HIDING IT IN HIS ROOM.

MOTHERRR! JASON PUT WORMS IN A CARAMEL CORN TUB!

JASON, GET IN HERE!

THEN HE HID IT UNDER HIS BED WHERE HE KNEW I'D FIND IT!

THEN HE LEFT HIS DOOR OPEN SO I'D SNEAK IN THERE AND LOOK FOR STUFF!

WHAT?

NEVER MIND.

...THEN HE SAID "DON'T GO IN MY ROOM" 'CAUSE HE KNEW THAT I WOULD...

CAN I HAVE SOME MONEY? MARCUS AND I ARE GONNA GO RENT A MOVIE.

WHAT MOVIE?

"BIG SLASHING MOMMAS WITH CHAIN SAW DAUGHTERS."

ABSOLUTELY NOT!

OK, OK, WE'LL JUST GET "SCARFACE."

MUCH BETTER.

I CAN'T BELIEVE SHE FELL FOR IT.

HURRY UP BEFORE SHE CATCHES ON.

IT IS A FAR, FAR BETTER THING THAT I DO, THAN I HAVE EVER DONE.

IT IS A FAR, FAR BETTER REST THAT I GO TO, THAN I HAVE EVER KNOWN.

AMEND

HEY! WHO BIT THE HEAD OFF MY RABBIT?!

MOM, CAN I BORROW YOUR CAR? I NEED TO GO OVER TO STEVE'S.

STEVE LIVES TWO BLOCKS AWAY— WHY CAN'T YOU WALK?!

I'LL FREEZE TO DEATH!

IT'S 50 DEGREES OUT. WEAR A SWEATER.

AMEND

I CAN'T. LAURIE PETERSON'S GONNA BE THERE. A SWEATER WOULD HIDE MY BULGING BICEPS.

LAURIE HAD **BETTER** APPRECIATE THIS...

WHAT ARE YOU READING?

"THE DICTIONARY OF CULTURAL LITERACY." I'M SICK AND TIRED OF FEELING STUPID.

DID YOU KNOW THAT DEMOSTHENES WAS THE GREATEST ORATOR OF ANCIENT GREECE? DID YOU KNOW THAT ALBERT SCHWEITZER WON THE NOBEL PEACE PRIZE? DID YOU KNOW THAT PYONGYANG IS THE CAPITAL OF NORTH KOREA?

AMEND

DID YOU KNOW YOU'RE SITTING ON IGUANA DROPPINGS?

DON'T SAY IT.

I GUESS YOU FEEL PRETTY STU—...

36

by Bill Amend

# FoxTrot

PHYSICS... FIZZIKS... PHISSIX... FIZZIQUES...

NO MATTER HOW YOU SPELL IT...

AARGH! I HATE THIS!

HOMEWORK GETTING YOU DOWN?

DAD, DO YOU KNOW ANYTHING ABOUT PHYSICS?

PHYSICS? ARE YOU KIDDING? I WAS THE **KING** OF PHYSICS BACK IN MY HEYDAY! WHAT'S THE PROBLEM?

AMEND

"CALCULATE THE PERIODIC CONSTANT, K, FOR THE SIMPLE HARMONIC MOTION OF A PARTICLE OF MASS m DROPPED INTO A FRICTIONLESS HOLE BORED THROUGH THE CENTER OF THE EARTH."

HMMMMM...

HMMMMM...

I'LL BE RIGHT BACK— I'VE GOTTA GO TO THE BATHROOM.

WHERE'S YOUR FATHER?

I THINK HE'S IN JASON'S ROOM.

OK, I FIGURED IT OUT...

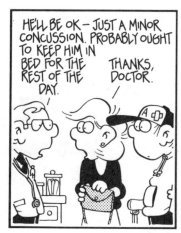

HERE YOU GO— I FOUND THESE IN THE ATTIC.

WHAT ARE THEY?

THEY'RE COMIC BOOKS YOUR BROTHER PETER MADE WHEN **HE** WAS YOUR AGE.

I THOUGHT THEY MIGHT GIVE YOU SOME IDEAS.

"BILLY THE BUTTERFLY"?

I'LL BET YOU DIDN'T KNOW YOUR BROTHER WAS SO TALENTED.

I DIDN'T KNOW MY BROTHER WAS SUCH A DWEEB.

AMEND

PAIGE, I NEED HELP WITH THE COVER OF MY COMIC BOOK, "SLUG-MAN BATTLES THE SEWER DEMON."

WHAT DO YOU NEED **ME** FOR?

I'M HAVING TROUBLE DRAWING IT.

DON'T LOOK AT ME—I CAN'T DR—...

SKETCH SKETCH SKETCH

MOTHERRR!

OOO—PERFECT! COULD YOU TURN A LITTLE TO YOUR LEFT?

SO WHAT DO YOU THINK?

WELL?

MOM?

WOW—MUST BE MORE ENGROSSING THAN I THOUGHT.

DROP THE "EN."

AMEND

by Bill Amend

FoxTrot

SORRY ABOUT THAT.

WHERE'D **HE** COME FROM?

HE WAS OUTSIDE. I THINK HE'S A STRAY.

ISN'T HE A **CUTE** LITTLE KITTY!

OH, PLEASE CAN WE KEEP HIM, MOM? PLEEEEASE?

I DON'T KNOW, PAIGE, WE—...

LOOK WHAT I FOUND OUTSIDE, JASON.

BLECH.

ZZZZ

AMEND

Meow.

OH, PLEASE CAN WE KEEP HIM, MOM? PLEEEEASE?

QUINCY! WAIT!

YOU CERTAINLY LOOK CHIPPER THIS MORNING.

I AM. TODAY'S THE DAY I GET TO TURN IN MY COMIC BOOK.

I SPENT A WHOLE WEEK DRAWING IT. IT'S THE BEST THING I'VE EVER DONE. I REALLY THINK MISS GRINCHLEY'S GONNA LIKE IT.

WHERE IS IT?

IT'S UP IN MY ROOM. WANNA SEE?

ABSOLUTELY.

OK— HOLD ON WHILE I GO GET IT...

START THE XXIII

SLUG-MAN

AMEND

HOLD ON— I'LL BE RIGHT BACK!

WHERE'S HE OFF TO?

HE'S GOING TO SHOW ME THE COMIC BOOK HE MADE.

MMM.

AAAAA!

SEEMS WE HAVE A DISTURBANCE IN THE NATURAL ORDER.

NATURALLY.

AMEND

JASON, HONEY, WHAT'S WRONG?

QUINCY ATE MY COMIC BOOK.

ALL OF IT?

EVERY PAGE. ALL THAT'S LEFT ARE CRUMBS COVERED WITH IGUANA SPIT.

AMEND

I'M SORRY, HONEY, BUT THAT'S WHAT HAPPENS WHEN YOU LEAVE THINGS WHERE QUINCY CAN GET AT THEM.

THAT COMIC BOOK WAS DUE TODAY!

I'M SURE MISS GRINCHLEY WILL—...

I KNEW I SHOULDN'T HAVE DRAWN SLUG-MAN SO REALISTICALLY!

47

SO, MOM, IS IT OK IF I PAY FOR THE TUX WITH YOUR CREDIT CARD?

YOU'RE SAYING THAT TO RUB IT IN, AREN'T YOU!

WHAT?!

YOU'RE RUBBING IN THE FACT THAT **YOU'RE** GOING TO THE PROM AND **I'M** NOT. GO AHEAD AND GLOAT— IT DOESN'T BOTHER ME IN THE LEAST.

AMEND

OBVIOUSLY.

BOOGER HEAD.

WHAT?

AREN'T YOU GOING TO ASK ME WHAT HAPPENED AT SCHOOL TODAY?

WHAT HAPPENED AT SCHOOL TODAY?

A JUNIOR ASKED **ME** TO THE PROM.

WHO?

CHRIS MORRISSEY.

AMEND

No! YES!

PAIGE, CHRIS MORRISSEY IS THE BIGGEST SLEAZE ARTIST IN THE SCHOOL!

BULL. YOU'RE JUST MAD I'M GOING TO YOUR STUPID PROM.

HE'S A LECH!

HE'S A JUNIOR AND HE ASKED **ME** TO BE HIS DATE.

AMEND

HE'S GOT HORMONES COMING OUT HIS EARS!

THERE I WAS, COMING OUT OF THE LIBRARY, WHEN HE POPPED UP AND ASKED ME. I MEAN, I WAS CAUGHT **COM-PLETELY** OFF GUARD!

GET USED TO IT.

I WONDER IF HE LIKES ME FOR MY CLEVER WIT. I **WAS** PRETTY FUNNY IN GYM CLASS...

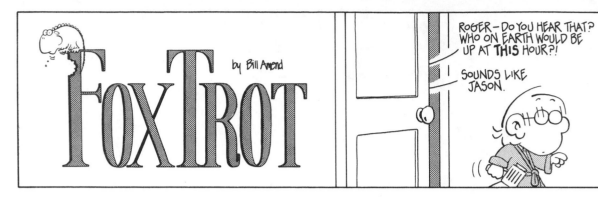

AAAAA!

56

MOM, WHERE'S DAD'S ELECTRONIC CHESS GAME?

WHY? I THOUGHT YOU SAID IT WAS TOO EASY FOR YOU.

ACTUALLY, I WANT TO SEE HOW IT WORKS.

JASON, I DON'T WANT YOU TAKING APART AND BREAKING YOUR FATHER'S CHESS THING!

I'M NOT GONNA TAKE IT APART AND BREAK IT! GEEZ!

IT'S IN THE HALL CLOSET.

...I'M JUST GONNA TAKE IT APART.

AMEND

WHAT ARE YOU DOING?

TAKING APART DAD'S ELECTRONIC CHESS GAME. WE'RE TRYING TO SEE HOW IT WORKS.

YOU'VE GOT TO BE KIDDING! EVEN I KNOW HOW IT WORKS!

YOU DO?

AMEND

YOU TURN IT ON AND IT PLAYS CHESS!

GEEZ — WHAT A MORON.

I'M SPEECH-LESS.

THEN CAN I SAY IT?...

OK, MARCUS, WE'RE ABOUT TO SEE WHAT MAKES AN ELECTRONIC CHESS GAME TICK...

WELL, FOR STARTERS, IT'S GOT BATTERIES...

TWO "D" CELLS, I'D SAY...

AMEND

59

by Bill Amend

PAIGE, YOU DIDN'T STAY UP ALL NIGHT, DID YOU??

I **HAD** TO, MOTHER— I'VE GOT MY GEOMETRY FINAL TODAY!

I'M OVER HERE.

OH.

10 MINUTES LEFT...

10 MINUTES LEFT AND I HAVEN'T DONE ONE PROBLEM!

THINK, PAIGE! THINK! THINK! THINK! THIS IS YOUR FINAL EXAM—YOUR GRADE IS ON THE LINE HERE!

THINK! THINK! THINK!

$c^2 = a^2 + b^2$

DEF'N OF ELLIPSE:
$\frac{x^2}{a^2} + \frac{y^2}{b^2} = 1$

$c = 2\pi r$

THINK! THINK!

$\tan\theta = \frac{b}{a}$

$V = \frac{4}{3}\pi r^3$

$\alpha' = \alpha'' \therefore \theta' = \theta''$ Q.E.D.

THINK! THINK! THINK!

SOH-CAH-TOA... OR IS IT TOH-CAH-SOA?...

$A = \pi r^2$

$\vec{a} \cdot \vec{b} = ab\cos\theta$

THINK! THINK!

NINE MINUTES LEFT...

AAAAA!

POOF!

WOW—WHAT A **HORRIBLE** NIGHTMARE!

BLINK BLINK BLINK

AMEND

TWO MINUTES LEFT...

RELATIVELY SPEAKING.

by Bill Amend

"OUT OF THE TOMB, WE BRING BADROULBADOUR, WITHIN OUR BELLIES, WE HER CHARIOT. HERE IS AN EYE. AND HERE ARE, ONE BY ONE, THE LASHES OF THAT EYE AND ITS WHITE LID."

YOU LIKE THIS— I CAN TELL.

YOU WOULDN'T BELIEVE WHAT JASON'S DOING.

WHAT?

HE'S READING POETRY TO HIS VENUS FLYTRAP.

YOU HAVE **GOT** TO BE KIDDING.

I'M SERIOUS. HE SAYS IT MAKES PLANTS GROW FASTER.

GET THIS: HE WANTS THE "MOUTHS" TO BE FIVE FOOT TWO IN DIAMETER. WHAT A GOOBER.

I'M FIVE FOOT TWO!

AHHH...

I THINK IT'S GROWING! LOOK!

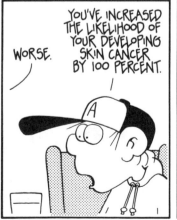

# FoxTrot

by Bill Amend

GUESS WHAT MOVIE OPENS FRIDAY?

JASON, I'M BUSY. I DON'T KNOW.

C'MON, GUESS.

JASON, I DON'T HAVE TIME FOR THIS.

AMEND

C'MON— YOU'LL NEVER GUESS.

"BATBOY."

"BAT-MAN"! BATMAN, MOTHER! WINGED DEFENDER OF THE PEOPLE OF GOTHAM!

YOU MIGHT WANT TO LOOSEN THAT HOOD JUST A LITTLE...

WHAT ARE YOU DOING?!

LOOKING AT YOUR WATCH.

THE FIRST SCREENING OF "BATMAN" STARTS IN TWO DAYS, ONE HOUR AND 49 SECONDS.

48... 47... 46...

I GUESS THERE'S A REASON WHY BATMAN DOESN'T WEAR GLASSES.

AMEND

WELL, WE'RE OFF.

HAVE FUN. WHAT THEATER ARE YOU GOING TO?

THE REGENCY. IT'S GOT 70mm THX SURROUND SOUND.

THAT'S IN THE CITY. WHO'S TAKING YOU?

AMEND

PETER.

NOW, YOU REALIZE HE'S DOING YOU A BIG FAVOR, SO I WANT YOU TO BE CONSIDERATE.

WE GOT YOU A BAT HAT.

JUST LIKE OURS.

SEE THIS THING DOWN HERE? IT'S CALLED A BRAKE PEDAL...

WHAT'S WITH DAD?

OH, HE'S JUST A LITTLE DEPRESSED.

BUT IT'S HIS BIRTHDAY!

I THINK HE'D RATHER IT WEREN'T. ALL THE HOOPLA'S RUBBING IN THE FACT THAT HE'S 45. HE'S FEELING OLD.

BUT HE'S GETTING PRESENTS! DON'T **THEY** CHEER HIM UP??!

I THINK HE'D RATHER NOT GET ANY PRESENTS.

GEEZ—HE'S NOT ONLY OLD, HE'S SENILE.

BLOW OUT THE CANDLES, DADDY.

THAT WAS PRETTY PATHETIC, DADDY.

PAIGE, FOR CRYING OUT LOUD—LOOK AT HOW MANY CANDLES HE HAD TO BLOW OUT!

ONE... TWO... THREE... FOUR... FIVE... SIX... SEVEN...

WE KNOW, JASON.

KISSES WON'T WORK, ANDY. I'M 45. I'M AN OLD MAN NOW.

YOU'RE WASTING YOUR TIME. I'M OVER THE HILL.

I'M **TELLING** YOU, I'M OVER THE... OVER THE... THE...

OH, WHAT THE HECK.

by Bill Amend

FOXTROT

Dear President Bush,
Will you *please* support legislation banning semiautomatic weapons?

Particularly the "squirt" variety.

EAT WATER, FROG LIPS.

BLAT BLAT BLAT

PAIGE, DO YOU KNOW ANYTHING ABOUT SQUIRT GUNS?

NOPE.

MAX FACTOR  Cosmopolitan

I JUST BOUGHT THIS BATTERY-POWERED REPEAT-ACTION WATER UZI AND IT'S NOT WORKING RIGHT.

LEMME SEE. WHAT'S WRONG WITH IT?

HMMMM...

THE AIM IS WAY OFF.

HEE HEE HEE...

GIVE IT A TRY.

BLAT BLAT BLAT BLAT BLAT BLAT

AMEND

I MEAN, WHAT **POSSIBLE USE** IS THERE FOR A GUN THAT SHOOTS BACKWARD?!

YOU GOT ME.

WHO WANTS TO DRIVE ME TO THE MALL?

ANYONE? ANYONE?

(WHO DOESN'T WANT ME TELLING MOM AND DAD WHAT TIME HE CAME HOME LAST NIGHT?)

LET'S NOT TAKE ALL DAY AT MACY'S THIS TIME. WHO WANTS TO BUY ME A NEW BLOUSE?

AMEND

I CAN'T BELIEVE MOM. WHAT'D SHE DO NOW?

SHE WON'T LET ME OUT OF THE HOUSE 'TIL MY ROOM'S CLEAN. JUST HIDE IT ALL IN THE CLOSET. THAT'S WHAT I DO.

PETER, I CAN'T DO THAT. EXCUSE ME, MR. ETHICAL.

AMEND

NO, I MEAN IT'S STILL GOT LAST YEAR'S JUNK IN IT. OK, OK, WELL, WHAT ABOUT UNDER YOUR BED?

"OH, WE'RE THE BOYS OF THE CHORUS, WE HOPE YOU'LL LIKE OUR SHOW; WE KNOW YOU'RE ROOTIN' FOR US, BUT NOW WE HAVE TO GO-O-O."

YOU'RE SINGING ALONG TO A STUPID CARTOON! WHAT?

IT'S BUGS BUNNY. I'M TRYING TO MEMORIZE THE WORDS TO ALL THE LOONEY TUNES. I KNOW ONE LOONEY GOON.

AMEND

NO NO— LOONEY TUNES. T-U-N-E-S. NO NO— LOONEY GOON. J-A-S-O-N.

THERE HAS **GOT** TO BE AN EASY WAY TO GET $40.

WHAT'S THIS?

IT'S AN ENVELOPE.

WITH MONEY IN IT.

AMEND

PENNIES FROM HEAVEN.

MORE LIKE 20s FROM HEAVEN.

$80, JASON! THIS ENVELOPE HAS $80 IN IT! YOU KNOW WHAT THAT MEANS?!

WE'RE RICH! WE'RE RICH! WE'RE RICH! WE'RE RICH!

I CAN BUY MY BASEBALL GLOVE!

AND I CAN BUY THE "INDIANA JONES" ACTION FIGURES ASSORTMENT PACK THAT I'VE WANTED ALL MY LIFE!

AMEND

I CAN BUY MY BASEBALL GLOVE! YES!

ALL THANKS TO EUGENE BLANKENSHIP.

WHO'S EUGENE BLANKENSHIP?

THE NAME ON THE ENVELOPE.

JASON, THERE'S A NAME ON THE ENVELOPE!

SO?

SO?! SO WE KNOW WHO THIS MONEY BELONGS TO.

SO?

AMEND

SO, YOU KNOW WHAT THAT MEANS, DON'T YOU?!

EUGENE BLANKENSHIP IS OUT 80 BUCKS?

NO, WE HAVE AN ETHICAL DILEMMA ON OUR HANDS.

I LIKE MY ANSWER BETTER.

HEY, KIDS—WHAT TIME IS IT!?

IT'S VACATION-TIME!

AND GUESS WHERE WE'RE GOING THIS YEAR!?

UNCLE RALPH'S CABIN, WHERE WE'VE GONE FOR THE PAST 10 SUMMERS.

HAWAII!

DAD, YOU'RE BLOCKING THE T— WHAT?!

AMEND

HAWAII! THINK ABOUT IT! SURFING...

SCUBA DIVING...

LYING IN THE SUN...

HULA DANCERS...

VOLCANOES...

LYING IN THE SUN...

JUNGLES...

SPEAR FISHING...

LYING IN THE SUN...

THE CHARCOAL REMNANTS OF OUR SISTER...

LYING IN THE SUN...

LYING IN THE SUN...

AMEND

WHATCHA WATCHING?

RERUNS OF "MAGNUM." I'M TRYING TO LEARN AS MUCH ABOUT HAWAII AS I CAN BEFORE WE GO.

THAT'S A GOOD IDEA.

FERRARIS, BIKINI-BABES AND HELICOPTERS —THIS PLACE IS GOING TO BE GREAT.

AMEND

THERE ARE ALSO HISTORIC LANDMARKS, WATERFALLS, A RICH NATIVE CULTURE AND WONDERFUL PLACES TO SHOP.

I FAST-FORWARD THROUGH THOSE.

I GUESS THEY DO DISTRACT FROM THE FERRARIS AND BIKINI-BABES.

WELL, I TRIED TO FAST-FORWARD THROUGH THE BIKINI-BABES TOO, BUT GEEZ—THEY'RE EVERYWHERE!

GUESS WHO'S GONNA BE A J.V. CHEERLEADER.

CONGRATULATIONS, PAIGE! WHEN DID YOU FIND OUT?

WELL, THEY HAVEN'T ACTUALLY SAID ANYTHING YET. TRYOUTS ARE ALL THIS WEEK.

YOU SOUND AWFULLY CONFIDENT, THOUGH.

AMEND

I'M A SHOO-IN, MOTHER. I'VE GOT THE KEY ATTRIBUTE.

WHAT'S THAT?

A BIG AIR POCKET BETWEEN HER EARS.

NO, I CAN **YELL,** YOU SNOT-BAG!

OUCH. THANK YOU, JASON.

...NOW A GENIUS LIKE ME, FOR INSTANCE WOULDN'T STAND A CHANCE...

AMAZING.

WHAT?

I JUST TOLD PETER I WAS TRYING OUT FOR CHEERLEADING AND HE WAS ACTUALLY SUPPORTIVE ABOUT IT.

ALL MY LIFE HE'S MADE FUN OF EVERYTHING I DO. I FIGURED HE'D MAKE ALL SORTS OF DUMB CHEERLEADER CRACKS, BUT HE DIDN'T. HE SAID "WAY TO GO, PAIGE!" CAN YOU BELIEVE IT?!

AMEND

UNFORTUNATELY, YES.

WHAT DO YOU MEAN?

YOU **WILL,** LIKE, INVITE ME TO PRACTICES, RIGHT?

PAIGE IS GONNA BE A CHEERLEADER.

GO! GO! GO TEAM, GO!

AMEND

GO! GO! GO TEAM, GO!

GO! GO! GO TEAM, GO!

PETER AND JASON ARE GONNA BE BASKET CASES.

NO NO— JASON'S GONNA BE LIVING WITH MARCUS.

GO! GO!

GO! GO!

...BUT WHAT IS HAWTHORNE **TELLING** US THROUGH THE JUXTAPOSITION OF THESE IMAGES? PAIGE?

DIMMESDALE DID IT, YES HE DID...

...HE'S THE FATHER OF HESTER'S KID!

CHEERLEADING TRYOUTS AREN'T FOR ANOTHER TWO HOURS, PAIGE.

I'M TRYING TO GET WARMED UP.

OK NEXT?

CHEERLEADER TRYOUTS 3 PM

C'MON, TEAM, MAKE 'EM FUME N' FUSS...

EADER OUTS PM

...SEND 'EM HOME LOSERS IN THEIR LOSER PUS!

DER S

—I MEAN BUS.

NEXT...

CHEERLEADER TRYOUTS 3 PM

I DIDN'T MAKE THE CHEERLEADING SQUAD.

OH, PAIGE, I'M SORRY.

OH, WELL. WHO WANTS TO BE A STUPID CHEERLEADER ANYWAY?! WHO WANTS EVERY GUY IN THE SCHOOL STARING AT HER LEGS AND LUSTING AFTER HER?! WHO WANTS TO BE THOUGHT OF AS "THAT CUTE BABE WITH THE POM-PONS"?!

I'D BETTER STOP BEFORE I GET DEPRESSED.

YOU'D BETTER STOP BEFORE I GET DEPRESSED.

# FoxTrot
by Bill Amend

LET'S SEE... RED ROLLED A FOUR, WHITE ROLLED A TWO...

LOOKS LIKE I GO FIRST.

WHAT ARE YOU DOING?

PLAYING BACKGAMMON.

RATTLE RATTLE RATTLE

BY YOURSELF?!

I LIKE TO PLAY ONLY SKILLED OPPONENTS.

CLUMP CLUMP CLUMP

WAIT A MINUTE— YOU JUST ROLLED SEVEN AND MOVED NINE. YOU'RE CHEATING!

SHHH. MY OPPONENT DIDN'T NOTICE.

RATTLE RATTLE RATTLE

YOU ARE SO WEIRD!

QUIET. I'VE GOT $1,000 RIDING ON THIS GAME. YEE-HAH! DOUBLE SIXES!

YOU ROLLED A THREE.

HE CHEATS, I CHEAT. LOOKS LIKE ANOTHER STROLL DOWN VICTORY LANE.

YOU ARE SUCH A LOSER!

LOSER NOTHING—I'M 22 AND 0.

AMEND

AAAAAAAAAAAA!

I DIDN'T KNOW YOU LIKED BACKGAMMON.

YOU MIGHT SAY I ENJOY PLAYING WITH PAIGE.

DAD SAYS YOU'RE GOING TO BE WRITING A COLUMN FOR THE NEWSPAPER.

UH HUH. IT'S ABOUT FAMILY LIFE IN THE '90s.

FICTIONAL FAMILY LIFE?

NO, REAL-LIFE EXAMPLES OF WHAT GOES ON IN THE HOME THESE DAYS.

SO IF I WERE TO, LIKE, THROW A STINK BOMB AT PAIGE, YOU'D MENTION IT IN THE COLUMN?

PROBABLY. WHY?

FAME-CITY HERE I COME.

I SAID WHY?!

SO HOW'S THE SOON-TO-BE-FAMOUS COLUMNIST DOING?

I JUST FINISHED THE FIRST ONE. WANNA SEE?

OF COURSE! WHAT'S IT ABOUT?

I THOUGHT I'D START BY DESCRIBING YOU GUYS TO THE READERS.

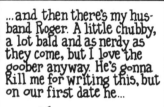

...and then there's my husband Roger. A little chubby, a lot bald and as nerdy as they come, but I love the goober anyway. He's gonna kill me for writing this, but on our first date he...

AAAAA!

WHAT?— IS THERE A TYPO?

HERE IT IS— HOT OFF THE PRESS.

LET'S SEE! LET'S SEE!

HEY, WAIT A MINUTE—THEY SPELLED MY NAME WRONG!

HOT BATMAN II RUMOR: AMEND TO PLAY NEW NEMESIS, "THE CARTOONIST" Megabucks Deal in Works

HOW SO?

THEY SPELLED IT "BOGER." IT LOOKS LIKE "BOOGER."

HONESTLY, ROGER —I'LL BET NO ONE EVEN NOTICES.

WHAT DO YOU MEAN? I DID...

KLEENEX, ANYONE?

SO HOW WAS SCHOOL TODAY?

MISERABLE.

IT WAS, WITHOUT EXAGGERATION, THE WORST DAY EVER IN MY 16 YEARS OF EXISTENCE!

AMEND

YOU WANT TO TALK ABOUT IT?

NO, I'D RATHER JUST TRY TO FORGET ABOUT IT.

OK, LET'S CHANGE THE TOPIC—DID ANY OF YOUR FRIENDS SEE MY COLUMN?

MOM, C'MON—I'M TRYING TO FORGET.

PETER, I'M WRITING A COLUMN ABOUT FAMILY LIFE. I **HAVE** TO MENTION YOU ONCE IN A WHILE.

WHY'S IT HAVE TO BE ABOUT **OUR** FAMILY?!

IT'S SUPPOSED TO RING TRUE—I CAN'T JUST MAKE EVERYTHING UP.

SAYS WHO?

SAYS MY EDITOR, FOR ONE.

YOUR EDITOR DOESN'T HAVE PEOPLE LAUGHING IN HIS FACE ALL DAY, SAYING WHAT A 'BOZO HE IS!

AMEND

YOU'RE RIGHT—IT'S MORE OR LESS BEHIND HIS BACK.

I MEAN, WRITE SOMETHING ABOUT **HIM** AND SEE HOW **HE** LIKES IT!

PETER WANTS ME TO ASK YOU IF HE CAN EAT OVER AT STEVE'S TONIGHT.

WHY CAN'T HE ASK ME HIMSELF?

YOU WROTE IN YOUR COLUMN THAT HE CRIED AT THE END OF "E.T." SO NOW HE'S NOT SPEAKING TO YOU.

WHAT IS IT WITH THAT BOY?! I MEAN, WHEN I WROTE ALL THAT STUFF ABOUT YOU PLAYING "DOCTOR" WITH TIMMY NORTH **YOU** DIDN'T STOP SPEAKING TO ME!

AMEND

I DIDN'T, DID I.

TELL HIM HE'S GETTING ALL WORKED UP OVER NOTHING.

PAIGE WANTS ME TO TELL YOU THAT PETER'S STILL UPSET.

MOM, ABOUT YOUR COLUMN—COULDN'T YOU JUST USE A PSEUDO-THINGIE LIKE "DEAR ABBY"?

A PSEUDO-NYM?

A FAKE NAME.

PAIGE, THE PROBLEM WITH A PSEUDONYM IS NO ONE KNOWS WHO WRITES IT.

EXACTLY.

WHAT'S WRONG WITH USING MY REAL NAME?

EVERYONE KNOWS WHO WRITES IT!

EVERYONE? YOU REALLY THINK SO? GOSH...GEE...

AMEND

DAD, YOU'VE GOT TO DO SOMETHING ABOUT MOM— SHE'S RUINING OUR LIVES!

WHAT DO YOU MEAN?

SHE'S WRITING PERSONAL STUFF IN HER COLUMN. LIKE ABOUT THE TIME SHE CAUGHT DENISE AND ME KISSING!

OR THE TIME MY BIRTHDAY CAKE CAUGHT MY HAIR ON FIRE.

HEE HEE—I THINK YOU GUYS ARE BEING A LITTLE TOO SENSITIVE. EVERYBODY HAS EMBARRASSING THINGS HAPPEN TO THEM.

LIKE THE TIME YOU FORGOT TO PUT THE SEAT DOWN ON THE TOILET AND GOT STUCK?

EXACTLY. WAIT A MINUTE... HOW'D YOU— ANDY!...

AMEND

OK, KIDS, YOU WIN. I'VE TALKED WITH MY EDITOR AND FROM NOW ON, MY COLUMN WILL BE WRITTEN UNDER A PEN NAME.

YAY!

AMEND

FROM NOW ON, IT WILL BE "ON THE HOME FRONT" BY ERMA LANDERS. I HOPE YOU'RE HAPPY.

YAY!

AND TO FURTHER ENSURE YOUR ANONYMITY, YOU ALL CAN HAVE PSEUDONYMS TOO.

YAY!

ANY SUGGESTIONS?

RAMBO.

RAQUEL.

PETER FOX.

**FoxTrot**

by Bill Amend

OK, IN THIS SCENE, THE GIANT MUTANT SWAMP BEAST DESCENDS ON THE CITY, EATS ALL THE PEOPLE, CRUSHES ALL THE BUILDINGS, BLOWS UP THE NUCLEAR REACTOR AND MAKES A GENERAL MESS OF THINGS.

WHAT'S HIS MOTIVATION?

SWAMP BEASTS DON'T NEED MOTIVATION.

JUST ASKING.

CRUSH! CRUSH! CRUSH!

GROWL! GROWL! GROWL!

EXXON

HELP ME! HELP ME! HELP ME!

BURP.

BOINK BOINK

WHAM! WHAM! WHAM!

OK, I THINK WE'RE READY FOR SOME CLOSE-UPS OF THE MONSTER.

WHAT DO YOU MEAN PAIGE WENT TO THE **MALL**!?

I **KNEW** WE SHOULD HAVE SHOT HER STUFF FIRST.

AMEND

**FoxTrot** by Bill Amend

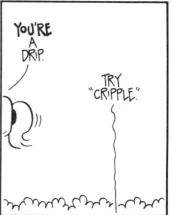